TINY HOUSES

TINY HOUSES

Sandra Leitte

TINY HOUSES

PRESTEL

Munich · London · New York

CONTENTS

INTRODUCTION

Simplicity boils down to two steps:
Identify the essential.
Eliminate the rest.

Leo Babauta, Zen Habits

Tiny houses – and living small – are hot topics. Many people find the idea appealing, to downsize, cut loose the ballast, perhaps even become more mobile while at the same time reducing their ecological footprint. Countless newspaper and magazine articles report on the trend, and television programmes accompany happy homeowners-to-be as they build their tiny house. People proudly show off their homes in online videos and discuss the advantages, and the disadvantages, of their chosen lifestyle. More life despite (or perhaps because of) fewer possessions – this is the philosophy behind the Tiny House Movement, which originated in the United States. The YouTube channel "Living Big in a Tiny House", which New Zealand actor and filmmaker Bryce Langston has run since 2013, shows how this can be achieved and what the reality of living in a reduced space actually looks like. Together with his partner Rasa Pescud, he travels around the world visiting people who have cut down their living space, be it in a camper van, tree house or a small home on wheels. With almost four million subscribers to the channel, it is clear how interested people are in the idea. But Bryce not only films and interviews tiny house owners, he is one himself. His fascination with tiny houses began when he was looking for a way to escape the expensive housing market in Auckland, New Zealand. He started to build his own tiny house in order to avoid high rents and give himself more freedom. Today he owns a tiny house on wheels of about 12 square metres (129 square feet), which he calls The Little Zen. He and Rasa live in it while they travel the United States for their YouTube show. They also have a small residence in New Zealand of around 15 square metres (161 square feet), also built on a trailer. This comparatively inexpensive way of living has enabled Bryce to devote himself entirely to his passion for small houses. In his online show, he tells the stories of people and their homes and gives insights into life in small spaces, sometimes even smaller than thought possible.

Take Kelly, for example, who built a tiny house near Wellington, New Zealand (see p. 86). After twenty years in the same job, she wanted a change. She sold her house with its three bedrooms and an expensive mortgage and moved into a 17-square-metre (183-square-foot) tiny house. There, thanks to the lower costs, she lives a simpler life, more flexible and with more time for things she cares about and enjoys. Her house, with an extreme minimalist design, can be run completely off-the-grid, thus making it easier to find a place to park it, as she is not dependent on a connection to the mains. Kelly now lives surrounded by nature, away from the big city, and enjoys her new home, which thanks to its reduced size combines high-quality materials and workmanship at an affordable price. She is very happy with her new job as a kindergarten teacher but is still considering reducing her working hours to just two or three days. Financially, she could easily afford it because of her low cost of living.

Optimised design

The Tiny House Movement is strongly influenced by a do-it-yourself mentality. Yet many architects and designers are also drawn to architecture on a reduced scale as both challenging and thrilling. The spatial requirements are completely different from those of a "normal" residential building. After all, the smaller space should in no way induce a lack of comfort or restricted use. For this reason, different spatial concepts must be developed for small-scale architecture. The young Italian architect Leonardo Di Chiara has succeeded in this with his tiny house aVOID (see p. 18). After graduating from university, he had no intention of settling down in a fixed location. So, it seemed an obvious choice for him to build a house on wheels in which he could enjoy a flexible and nomadic lifestyle. aVOID consists of a single empty room in which all the furniture and fittings are stored away in the walls. This takes a principle often applied to tiny houses to the extreme – flexible, multifunctional areas often replace rigidly assigned uses of space. This is achieved, for example, through movable structural elements and furniture or even foldable and collapsible fixtures. In Leonardo's 9-square-metre (97-square-foot) home, for instance, the dining room is created by folding the table and chairs out of the wall, while the bed is folded down in the evening.

All in all, the interaction between a home and its inhabitants is much closer in a tiny house, as every corner is put to maximum use or can be freely adapted by the inhabitants to their needs. Their relationship with their surroundings is usually also closer, as many of the houses are designed so the view outside visually expands the confined interior. Many such tiny houses are located in the middle of nature and the surrounding openness provides a generous sense of space.

And yet, especially in dense urban areas, small-scale building is a challenge to be met, increasingly becoming a topic of conversation. A shortage of housing and space and the rising prices of real estate in large cities demand a solution. Attempts have been made in this respect through projects that make use of small gaps between buildings and leftover plots, such as The Slot House in London (see p. 176) and a Skinny House in Osaka (see p. 196). In contrast, Casa Parásito (see p. 36) in Quito was built on the unused roof of an existing building. The modular construction is intended to demonstrate possibilities for cost-effective re-densification in the city and to encourage responsible, resource-saving consumption.

Small buildings as a field of experimentation

Tiny houses are particularly suitable for conducting architectural trials and experiments. They can be used to test new types of construction and materials, try out unconventional spatial distributions or discover unusual locations – high up in the mountains (see p. 52) or even on distant planets (see p. 30). Themes such as sustainability and putting a halt to climate change play an important role here. The architecture collective Refunc, for example, has specialised in working with materials that others regard as waste – such as old car tyres and wooden pallets or discarded silos. Hortus Hermitage (see p. 58) was created from two fibreglass silos, combined with repurposed materials from Groningen's botanical garden where the accommodation is located. For Refunc there is no rubbish, everything is part of the closed-loop cycle and reused accordingly. This conserves resources and, in doing so, the environment.

Construction materials companies also use small buildings for their materials research. A glass manufacturer, for example, built an extremely energy-efficient house entirely of glass in the Gorafe desert of Spain (see p. 96). This allows the individual properties of specially engineered glass to be tested in practice.

There is no official definition for tiny, micro, mini or small houses in most countries. In the United States, however, the dimensions provided by the International Residential Code have been enshrined in building regulations. They state that a house is considered "tiny" if it has a floor area of less than 37 square metres (400 square feet), without counting any lofts, while "small" houses generally include those with a floor area between 37 and 93 square metres (400 and 1,000 square feet). This is also the criterion that guided the selection of projects in this book.

Many of the examples presented here are only intended as temporary accommodations, as a holiday home or a place to rest and catch one's breath. Few people dare take the somewhat radical step of adopting a tiny living arrangement. But maybe a holiday in a tiny house would be a good way to find out just what it is like to live in a minimalist home reduced to the bare essentials?

For all those who dream of this alternative lifestyle, this book offers a variety of ideas to get you started. It inspires you to dive into the world of small living, where big rooms and lots of possessions count less than immaterial things like time, independence, financial freedom and eco-consciousness. The tiny house phenomenon redefines what makes a house a home. Bryce Langston says of his home, The Little Zen, "While to some my home may not seem like much, to me it's perfect. It meets all my basic needs and plenty of my desires. [. . .] It's absolutely enough."[1] With this house on wheels, he can be at home anywhere, anytime.

1 Bryce Langston, *Living Big in a Tiny House* (Nelson: Potton & Burton, 2018).

WOOLHOUSE

Csóromfölde, Hungary

Au Workshop + Marton Low

3 m²

32 ft²

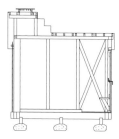

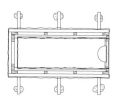

Sheep's wool is ideally suited as a natural material for insulation in construction. In winter it provides good thermal insulation, and in summer it protects the interior from excessive heat. Usually the insulant is hidden behind cladding, but this building leaves the two layers of wool visible. The tiny shelter was created as part of the Hello Wood International Summer School and Festival, an annual event in which architects from the world over develop and implement projects in collaboration with students. In 2018, the event was held under the motto "Cabin Fever".

The basic structure of woolhouse consists of a pine frame supported on stones. The washed and roughly combed wool is woven between the vertical wooden beams as in a weaving frame. The outer layer serves the protective function of keeping out both rain and pests. Even if the first layer gets wet, the inner layer remains dry and clean. A prefabricated, stepped aluminium roof closes the building off at the top, taking advantage of the chimney effect to conduct warm air up and out of the structure. From here, daylight also falls into the room through a skylight. Inside woolhouse there is space for just one person, either lying or sitting, on a wool mat with a wool pillow, of course. Behind the design is the idea of a "psychic ablution", a therapeutic space to let go of mental ballast. Accordingly, the small seat, which is mounted on the inside of the door, is meant to represent the place of an imaginary therapist. Surrounded by natural materials, their specific odour and individual feel, you may enjoy the silence of the room and retreat from everyday life.

HIDDEN STUDIO

Valencia, Spain
Fernando Abellanas

4 m²

43 ft²

Designer Fernando Abellanas has created a truly unusual workspace in the Spanish port city of Valencia. In a place that he keeps to himself, he has concealed a 2 × 2-metre (6.5 × 6.5-feet) refuge in the graffiti-covered concrete base of a road bridge. The metal and plywood construction hangs with casters from the bridge's girders and can be moved with the help of a hand winch – from the entry side, from which Abellanas mounts the platform, to the supporting pile where his "office" is located. It is furnished with a plastic chair, wooden shelves and a tabletop, all of which are firmly attached to the concrete wall. The mobile floor rolls under the furniture. And just in case it gets too late, a lamp and bedding are stored on one of the shelves.

For this self-taught designer who creates furniture under the name Lebrel, the many unnoticed, unused spaces in urban landscapes are great sources of inspiration. Most people pass them by without noticing. Abellanas, however, sees their potential for architectural interventions that provide them with a function. He compares his hideout to that feeling in childhood, when you hid under the table at a family gathering – protected, away from the hustle and bustle and yet in the middle of the action, simultaneously close and far away. In times when space in our cities is becoming scarce, this perspective on pre-existing niches can certainly reveal plenty of places that could be used for unconventional architectural extensions.

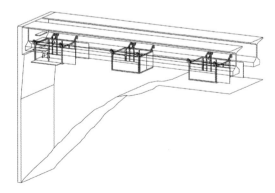

aVOID

Pesaro, Italy

Leonardo Di Chiara

9 m²

97 ft²

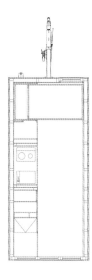

The name of the tiny house on wheels, designed by Italian architect Leonardo Di Chiara directly after his studies, refers to the void within. With external dimensions of just 5.10 × 2.50 metres (16.5 × 8 feet), aVOID is very small, even for a tiny house, despite a total height of 4 metres (13 feet). But the minimalist design of the interior allows for the space to be used in a multifunctional fashion, thereby accommodating all the requirements for living in a space of 9 square metres (97 square feet). All the furniture can be folded out of the walls – the bed and table, for example – or stored in it, such as the two folding chairs. One side consists entirely of cupboards and drawers. This is where the kitchenette, with fridge, sink, induction cooker and extractor fan, is accommodated. At the front by the entrance there is a bathroom of just 0.80 square metres (8.5 square feet) containing a composting toilet, folding washbasin and shower. It is lined throughout with Gaboon plywood. A particular highlight is the miniature

greenhouse for growing herbs, which is located under one of the skylights that illuminate the space. And should you ever feel cramped, you can enjoy the sun and the view from the accessible roof.

The narrow entrance side is completely covered with glass and uses solar radiation to passively heat the interior. This is just one of the structure's sustainable energy concepts, alongside the photovoltaic system with a storage battery for the power supply, controlled ventilation, infrared heating and energy-efficient appliances.

aVOID was created in cooperation with Tinyhouse University in Berlin and built with the support of Italian and German companies, who provided building materials for the project.

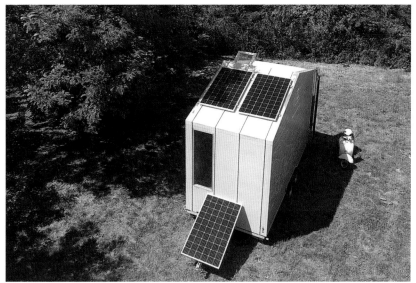

ASHEN CABIN

Ithaca, New York, USA
HANNAH Design Office

9 m²

97 ft²

The emerald ash borer, originally native to East Asia, was introduced into the United States in the early 2000s where it poses a massive threat to the local ash tree population. The infested trees were previously unusable as construction timber, in part because of the irregularly shaped trunks. As a result, the wood either rots in the forest or else it is used as firewood, releasing the CO_2 stored in the tree back into the atmosphere. Leslie Lok and Sasa Zivkovic of HANNAH Design Office both teach at Cornell University. Together with a group of students, they have developed a way to use the diseased ash wood, which is otherwise regarded as waste, in construction. For them, it provides a tremendous source of raw material for sustainably building with wood. In order to saw the logs to size, they designed a special tool from an industrial robot arm equipped with a bandsaw that produces naturally curved boards in various thicknesses. For Ashen Cabin, these were used as cladding both inside and out, creating a panel with insulation sandwiched between the wood.

Another innovative technology used to create the foundation and the 6.50-metre (21-foot)-high chimney was 3D printing with concrete. This process requires only the minimum amount of concrete that is structurally necessary, and no formwork is needed. In this way both material and energy are conserved.

The cabin's interior is extremely minimalist – the only piece of furniture is a wooden bench with a concrete base that serves as storage space. When needed, the bench can be converted into a place to sleep. A tiny kitchen with a small washbasin and shelf is right next to the door. The structure can be heated using an open fire. The floor features a charming pattern since the lines created by 3D printing have been left visible. The door and windows are highlighted both inside and out by black casing. They frame selective views of the surroundings and, above all, allow light to enter at all times of the day.

MARS CASE

Beijing, China
OPEN Architecture

129 ft²

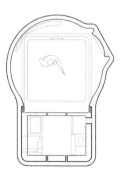

What do we really need to live? This was the question posed by architects Li Hu and Huang Wenjing of OPEN Architecture in an era of mass consumption, pollution and climate change. With their prototype for minimalist living, they explore how a dependence on natural resources can be minimised and one's living environment simplified.

Their ideas started with life on Mars, where the reuse and recycling of resources such as air, water, food and even waste would be essential for survival. Working together with a Chinese electronics giant, they developed a house on the basis of this concept that functions as a closed system – used air, waste water and waste heat are fed back into the system, thus reducing the consumption of resources.

They have packaged this technology within a two-part structure. There is the rectangular service module made of aluminium, which houses the kitchen, bathroom and all technical equipment and serves as storage space and airlock. When the door on the other side is opened, the bubble-shaped second module unfolds, which acts as the living space. A special membrane is being devised to be used as the material for this, simulated in the prototype in Beijing by a hard synthetic resin shell. A 2 × 2-metre (6.5 × 6.5-foot) area of floor is meant to adapt to the time of day, transforming into a hard surface during the day and a soft bed at night. Here too, materials research is still pending. Round windows in the vaulted outer skin offer views of the sky, the stars and perhaps even the distant planet Earth.

For transport, the inflatable part can be folded and stored in the service module – like in a suitcase, hence the name of the project. Compact, mobile, self-sufficient in terms of energy – a contribution to futuristic living on other planets but also food for thought today for life on earth.

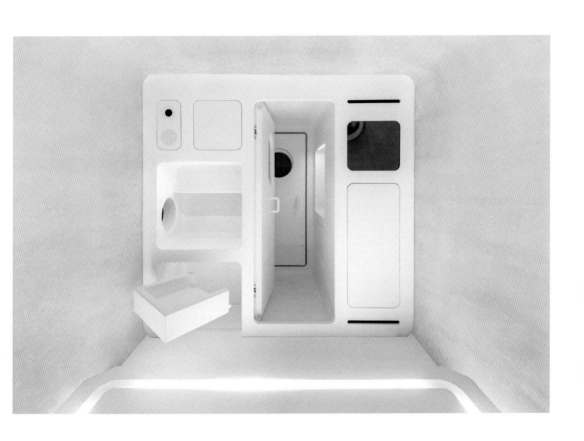

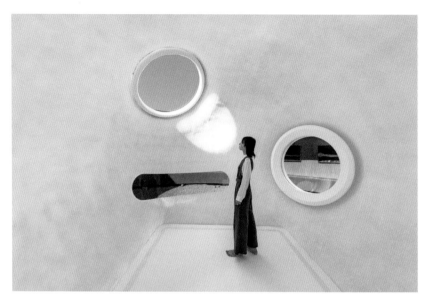

CASA PARÁSITO

Quito, Ecuador
El Sindicato Arquitectura

12 m²

129 ft²

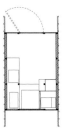

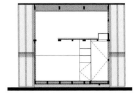

In biology, parasites are bacterial, plant or animal species that obtain their food by existing off another living creature, often harming it in the process. Casa Parásito in the Ecuadorian capital Quito, however, inflicts no damage at all. But it does draw its resources from a "host" by connecting to an existing supply of electricity and water, as well as the sewerage system. The architects of El Sindicato Arquitectura consider the small house on the roof of an extant building as a contribution to urban re-densification that conserves resources with a minimum of effort.

With a floor area of 2.50 × 3.60 metres (8 × 12 feet), the living space is minimalist, yet it covers every necessity: living area, kitchen and bathroom on the lower level, while the sleeping area is on a platform above. Since the roof extends down to around hip-level, it was important to provide an area for movement in the middle with sufficient ceiling height. All activities that take place standing up are carried out here. Work surface, table and storage space are located beneath the inclined roof.

The building consists of individual modules, designed as a wooden frame construction. Plenty of light enters the space through the large north-facing window. It also offers an impressive view over the city as far as the four distant volcanoes. The façade in the south admits light thanks to the frosted glass, while at the same time protecting those inside from the neighbours' view. The two longer sides and the roof are completely closed in order to keep down heat from solar radiation. The exterior is clad with steel panels, while OSB panels cover the interior. The space in between is 12 centimetres (about 5 inches) of eco-friendly coconut-fibre insulation.

The structure is inhabited by one of the architects of El Sindicato Arquitectura. Living in the tiny house has shown him what little material possessions he really needs to live, and it ensures that he is far more aware of his home and the everyday rituals that take place in it.

THE CABIN

near Brno, Czech Republic

Jan Tyrpekl

12 m²

129 ft²

Thousands of concrete bunkers stand in the border regions of the Czech Republic – relics of the Czechoslovak border fortifications. This defensive system was erected along the country's borders in the 1930s to protect against possible invasion by Nazi Germany. Many of the bunkers have slowly fallen into ruin, while a few have thankfully found a new purpose – as a museum, for example, or as the foundation for a retreat with a view, as is the case here. With his experimental wooden structure, architect Jan Tyrpekl sought to contribute to the discussion on how these historic military buildings might be used today.

A light wooden structure now extends upwards atop a concrete bunker, largely buried underground. It offers some 12 square metres (129 square feet) of space on two different levels. Large windows allow for a sweeping view over the fields and forests of the surrounding South Moravian landscape – on one side to the Austrian border, on the other to the nearest village. In a two-storey space, featuring a glass roof, a ladder leads to the upper level. This allows a generous amount of daylight to flood the room, while also extending the views upwards into the sky.

One of the principles behind the wooden tower was to keep the use of materials, costs and construction time to a minimum. The structure is simple and could be removed at any time without leaving a noticeable trace. The construction was carried out by hand, using ordinary tools, but it was only possible thanks to the active help of friends, family and architecture students who participated in the project. Now the building is open to the general public and may be used by anyone for a short-term stay.

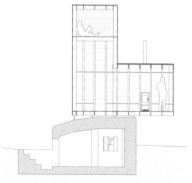

HAMMERFEST HIKING CABINS

Hammerfest, Norway
SPINN Arkitekter; Format Engineers

14 m²

151 ft²

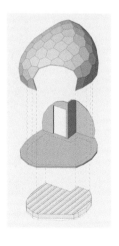

"Midnight sun, arctic nature and the northernmost town in the world – Welcome to Hammerfest!" With this slogan, the small Norwegian town by the sea situated north of the Arctic Circle advertises itself. To make hiking in the challenging but overwhelmingly beautiful surroundings more accessible, the Norwegian Trekking Association (DNT) has built two simple refuges here. The Norwegian architecture studio SPINN was commissioned to work out a prototype. Their sketches envisaged an organically shaped "rock" that would fit harmoniously into the harsh environment while disturbing it as little as possible. With the help of the British engineering firm Format, the design was then translated into a wooden construction consisting of 77 individual parts. Like a 3D jigsaw puzzle, the flat pentagonal and hexagonal elements fit together to form a curved double-shell of virtually maintenance-free Kebony wood. This is produced in a process developed in Norway, in which FSC certified pine wood is treated with furfuryl alcohol to increase its resilience

and durability – something of crucial importance in the harsh environment of northern Norway. In preparation the design underwent intensive testing in simulations of arctic storms and snowdrifts.

As the proposal exceeded the budget of the hiking club, the required capital was raised through a crowdfunding campaign. Local companies donated material and know-how, but it was the countless hours of volunteers that made the project possible. The cabin was prefabricated in a warehouse and then transported in two parts to its final location on Storfjellet.

Inside, the accommodation has minimal furnishings – benches, tables and a wood-burning stove. The natural pine creates a warm and cosy atmosphere. Through a large panoramic window, hikers can enjoy fantastic views of the mountainous surroundings and the North Sea while recovering from the exertion of their climb.

ON MOUNTAIN HUT

Piz Lunghin, Switzerland
BMCO Product Design; On Running

14 m²

151 ft²

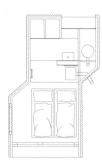

On the Lunghin Pass in the Swiss canton of Grisons, there is a rare sight to behold: The intersection of three continental watersheds lies at the very top of the pass. From here the water flows northwest into the Rhine, which flows into the North Sea, east into the Inn and over the Danube into the Black Sea, and finally southwest into Lake Como and via the Po into the Mediterranean. Below the pass lies the lake, Lägh dal Lunghin. Here, in the summer of 2019, a Swiss running shoe company constructed a self-sufficient, mobile alpine hut. The lodge can only be reached on foot, which meant that a standard construction process was not possible. Instead, the hut was prefabricated in the valley and the parts were flown to the site by helicopter. The structure was up and running in only three hours.

The floor is staggered across several levels in order to accommodate the angle of the slope. There is a recreation area, washing area, composting toilet and storage space. A wood-burning stove provides cosy warmth and can also be used as a cooker. A ladder leads to the sleeping area above in the two-storey structure facing the valley. Breathtaking views of the Engadine landscape can be enjoyed from the bed as well as through the large glass front below.

The hut is a modular construction made from laminated spruce veneer lumber left exposed in the interior. The mountains are reflected in the outer metal shell so that the hut blends in perfectly with its surroundings. The sustainability of On Mountain Hut was an important consideration for the clients. The power supply is provided by a solar panel with battery, a fresh-water tank can be filled at the lake or directly at the spring, and the waste water is filtered and recycled into nature. Moreover, the refuge can be dismantled again without leaving a trace in the landscape. With their minimalist shelter, the company founders hope not only to express their own love of the mountains but also to create a perfect place for a needed hiatus.

HORTUS HERMITAGE

Haren (Groningen), Netherlands

Refunc – Denis Oudendijk and Jan Körbes;
Sjaak Langenberg & Rosé de Beer

14 m²

151 ft²

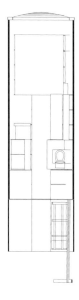

Hermits live isolated from society, often in remote, modest dwellings, also called hermitages. In their original sense, hermits were Christians who led a secluded life of prayer. But in the 18th century came the curious phenomenon of the garden hermit – "professional" hermits who were hired to reside in English country parks, living in specially built hermitages, and meant to show themselves at certain points of the day for the enjoyment of guests. In a way, the Hortus Hermitage combines both historical models. It serves as a contemplative retreat for self-discovery and meditation but is by no means secluded, situated as it is in the middle of the botanical gardens of Haren. The idea of allowing guests to spend the night in the gardens came from the artist duo Sjaak Langenberg and Rosé de Beer. The studio Refunc worked with them to design a minimalist accommodation made from a former sugar silo. Spatially and materially limited to bare essentials, the refuge is mainly made up of recycled materials: old garden benches have

been transformed into multifunctional seating that can be turned into a bed at night, while a desk became the kitchen countertop. Wall lamps have been created from seed trays and green plant tags now cover a desktop.

The funnel of the fiberglass silo was cut off for the entrance. Since Refunc likes to work in such a way that no residual material is left over, the funnel was put to use again to create a cone of light for the skylight, which illuminates the interior while allowing a view of the starry sky at night. At the end of the silo, too, light enters through a large porthole. A solar panel supplies the structure with electricity. A second, shorter silo houses a small kitchen with cooking facilities and a sink.

Those who stay at the Hortus Hermitage have the unique opportunity to experience the park outside opening hours, and those who wish to do so are welcome to make themselves useful and lend a hand.

59

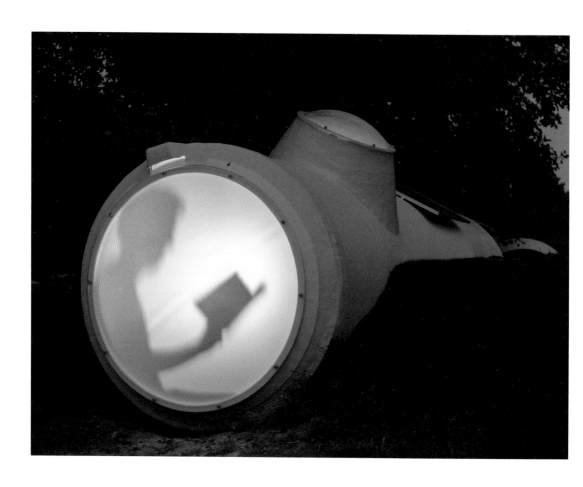

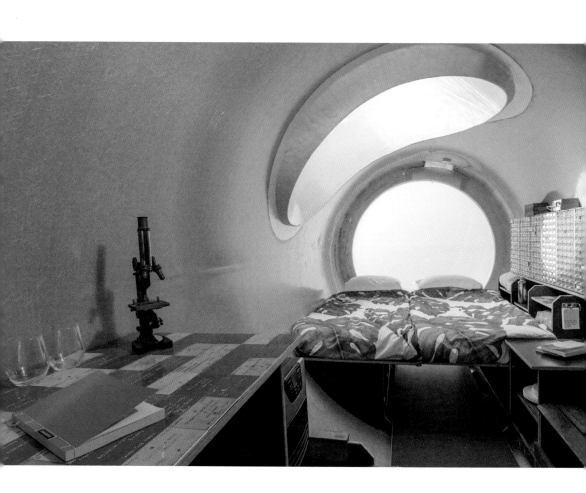

BASE CABIN

Melbourne, Australia
Studio Edwards; Base Cabin

15 m²

161 ft²

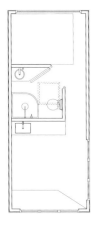

Whether in the open countryside, on the beach, in the city or in your own garden, Base Cabin offers you a retreat – a place to take a break from your everyday routine, regardless of where you are. Australian company Base Cabin, which specialises in small houses and cottages, commissioned Melbourne-based design and architecture firm Studio Edwards to create a design that would offer both functional and flexible living spaces and provide a fresh look at the design of tiny houses. The result is a sculptural creation with clean edges and clear forms, sloping, asymmetrical roof surfaces and a continuous, uniform exterior cladding of black rubber. The interior appears light and comfortable compared to the dark exterior. This is achieved by the wall panelling made of marine plywood, a high-quality wood-based material used in ship building, and the cedar flooring. Selectively slotted openings in the shell ensure maximum exposure to light. Through a skylight, natural daylight even reaches the centrally located bathroom, whose walls do not run completely to the

ceiling. The wet room, which also houses the kitchenette, divides the room into two parts: the living and sleeping areas. Above the bed, the roof is sloped like a tent, creating a cosy sleeping corner. A triangular window, which takes up the structure's entire gable side, affords a view to the outside. A wide bench in the living area may be converted into a second bed if required. The ceiling height here rises to 3.30 metres (11 feet), creating a feeling of spaciousness. This is reinforced by the large French door, which can be fully opened to extend the room to the outside.

The modern cabin is mounted on a trailer and is thus mobile. To ensure that the 6-metre (19.5-foot)-long and 2.30-metre (7.5-foot)-wide construction is not too heavy, the architect opted for an asymmetrical structure, which compared to straight walls reduces the use of materials.

FOREST CABIN

Slootdorp, Netherlands
The Way We Build

15 m²

161 ft²

Flat marshland won through dyke building and drainage systems on the North Sea coast is known as *koog* or polder. The Robbenoordbos, the "seal forest" where this wood-panelled cabin is located, is also found on land created in this manner. Although the area was originally drained around 1930, in April 1945 the occupying German troops blew up the protective dyke and the flooding torrents of water destroyed everything there. However, reconstruction began in May of the same year and by December 1945 the polder was dry once again. Since the area's north-eastern corner was found to be less suitable for agriculture, the area was forested. The place where seals once sunned themselves on sandbanks is now home to a young forest rich in biodiversity. A committed couple chose this location to establish the ecologically oriented campsite Het bos roept! – The Forest Is Calling! Among the permanent accommodations is the Forest

Cabin of Amsterdam architecture firm The Way We Build, founded by Arjen Aarnoudse and Farah Agarwal.
The entire structure of the cabin is built of poplar plywood, a fast-growing, locally sourced tree species. Arching structural elements define the space. Along the walls they extend down to the floor, as they do in the middle of the cabin demarcating the sleeping niche. A kind of dome is created in the centre, lending the accommodation a chapel-like atmosphere: an appropriate association since the architects intended to create a place of tranquillity to meditate and leave all worries behind. The cabin has a bed, small kitchen, wood-burning stove and composting toilet. Showers are available in the campsite. Through two fully glass-paned sides, guests get to feel wonderfully close to the forest and the surrounding nature and enjoy a break from city life.

REFUGE LE PIC MINEUR

Poisson Blanc Regional Park, Quebec, Canada
L'Abri

Ready for island living? Instead of heading south, it might be time to look north. In Canada's Poisson Blanc Regional Park, north of Ottawa, you can take a holiday on your very own island. Most of the campgrounds can only be reached by kayak or canoe and are therefore completely isolated in the wooded wilderness. A mere ten-minute walk from the campsite brings you to the cabin at the end of the promontory, Pointe de la Truite, designed and built by Montreal-based architects L'Abri.

The simple, almost sculptural accommodation blends in harmoniously with the wooded surroundings. The cedar panelling, which is acquiring a grey patina with time, and the metal roof, intended to mirror the agricultural buildings in the area, give the house a rustic charm. Inside, every necessity is housed in a single space: on the lower level there is the kitchenette, the dining area and the wood-burning stove with a chair hanging from the ceiling. A ladder leads up to the sleeping loft, which has just enough room for a queen size mattress. This second level is suspended from the ceiling by steel rods. Below, the dining table can be converted into another queen size bed when needed. The interior is also largely in wood, with black elements adding that certain *je ne sais quoi* to the micro shelter.

The focus of the light-flooded room, nevertheless, is on the large windows with their view of the surrounding nature and the lake. A roofed terrace extends the rather limited space inside into the outdoors – which is the main attraction of this location with its wide range of outdoor activities after all!

MINI LIVING URBAN CABIN

Beijing, China
MINI Living with penda China

15 m²

161 ft²

Hutongs are traditional Chinese residential areas that include courtyards and alleyways, which made up large parts of the urban landscape, especially in Beijing. They connect private spaces with public places for gatherings of those living there. Unfortunately, in recent decades they have been disappearing with increasing frequency to make way for modern multi-storey apartment blocks. Architect Sun Dayong of penda China decided to incorporate this architectural heritage into his design for the MINI Living Urban Cabin. The aim of MINI Living is to investigate how, in view of the current housing shortage and lack of space in large cities, a better quality of life can be achieved in a very small area of no more than 15 square metres (161 square feet). Following similar projects by the automotive company in London, New York and Los Angeles, this was to be the fourth Urban Cabin. In each case, the design department at MINI Living planned two of the three formal elements – one with a living and sleeping area, the other with a bathroom and kitchen. The third element is an experimental space designed by local architects.

The house consists of two square areas that are at an angle to each other. These are the elements created by MINI Living. Here you will find creative design ideas such as revolving sections of wall and fold-out furniture that allow for flexible use of the spaces. An open area at the front, which is covered by a semicircular roof, connects the two rooms. Here Sun Dayong has created a communal area as a modern interpretation of the traditional hutong, with a swing inviting people to sit down and spent time together. An unusual architectural element is the periscope-like roof structures, reminiscent of the densely packed houses of a hutong. Their golden covering reflects light. The reflective material can also be found in the wedge-shaped open space at the rear of the building. Inside, the walls' plywood panelling defines the space's material quality, complemented by the white surfaces of the columns and ceilings in contrast to the dark concrete floor, kitchenette and bed.

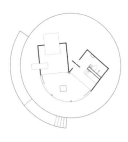

FIRST LIGHT TINY HOUSE

near Wellington, New Zealand
First Light Studio; Build Tiny

17 m²

183 ft²

Small houses built on a trailer are most often created as cost-saving do-it-yourself projects and are therefore more practical and functional than architecturally sophisticated. The Tiny House of the same name designed by the New Zealand firm First Light Studio shows that does not need to be the case. The client was looking for an elegant accommodation on wheels that would not compromise on design despite the strict requirements regarding dimensions and weight. The architects designed a 7.20-metre (23.5-foot)-long and 2.40-metre (8-foot)-wide sculptural form that the construction company Build Tiny executed as a steel frame structure on a twin axle trailer. On the outside, it is clad with black corrugated metal, while the inside is covered with light-coloured plywood. The furniture and fixtures are also made of this material. To make efficient use of the space and keep the room tidy and clean, storage areas are concealed in every corner: in drawers under the sliding sofa and the cupboards about it, and under the stairs. The kitchenette and the bathroom also offer plenty of space for every necessity. At the end of the kitchen unit there is a fold-out table that serves as an additional work surface and a place to eat. The bed is located in the loft illuminated by natural light from a large skylight. The highest point of the asymmetrical roof is located above the head of the bed so that the upper level can also be used in the most efficient way.

As the First Light Tiny House is equipped with solar panels complete with storage battery, it can be operated independently of the mains supply. Cooking is done with gas. Thanks to the composting toilet, no connection to the sewerage system is necessary, and the grey water can even be filtered and used for watering a garden.

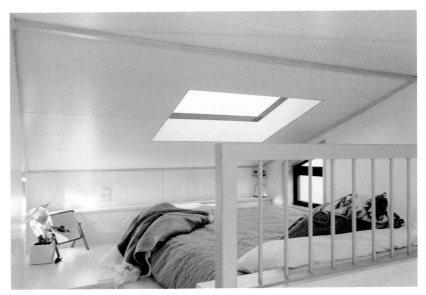

HYTTE NO. 1

Blankenhain, Germany
KOOP Architects; KOOP Mobile Timber Constructions

18 m²

194 ft²

Wood is a renewable resource which is particularly sustainable when raw materials are sourced from local forests. In addition, this natural building material ensures a healthy, balanced indoor climate, above all when left untreated and allowed to "breathe". The Thuringian company KOOP took advantage of this when building its first tiny house. They developed a completely wooden home on wheels, which they named Hytte, in reference to the Norwegian word for a cabin or holiday cottage.

From the outside, the 7-metre (23-foot)-long and 2.55-metre (8.5-foot)-wide mobile home stands out because of its rounded shape. The outer cladding is made of Kebony wood, which is weather-resistant and durable. With time it will develop a beautiful grey patina. You enter the mini house through a spacious French door. Behind it is the living and dining area which, thanks to the flexible furnishings, can be adapted to individual needs. The walls covered in light spruce make everything look bright and inviting. The well-thought-out green designer

kitchen adds a fresh accent of colour. The kitchenette and bathroom form a narrow passage leading to the rear of the accommodation. There, a small work area with skylight and built-in shelves encourages creativity and relaxation. A ladder leads up to the sleeping area, which opens generously toward the sky through a skylight.

The refuge is heated by a built-in wood-burning stove, supplemented by an energy-saving infrared heating system. The necessary electricity is provided by either the solar system mounted on the roof or, alternatively, via a connection to the power grid. In the bathroom there is a self-sufficient separating toilet, which works without water. If desired, the house can also be connected to the sewerage system. The water supply may be provided either by the public mains or from a water tank.

LA CASA DEL DESIERTO

Gorafe, Andalusia, Spain
OFIS Arhitekti

20 m²

215 ft²

A free-standing glass house in a region where people traditionally build their homes in caves to escape the extreme climate? The idea seems crazy. But an international glass manufacturer was curious. The aim was to show that their products could be used to construct buildings with a high quality of living even under the most challenging conditions. The team found an ideal location for the experiment in the desert of Gorafe in the Andalusian province of Granada. The area offers breathtaking landscapes and a starry sky unaffected by light pollution, but it is also considered one of the most hostile places in Europe, thanks to persistent drought and the extreme temperatures.

The Slovenian architects of OFIS Arhitekti were commissioned to design the desert house. An insulated construction of wooden boards covered with reflective panelling forms the roof and structural base of the building, which seems to float off the ground. Set between them is the actual building made of supporting glass walls. The three main areas are arranged in a Y-shape – the bedroom, sitting room and bathroom with a recessed bath – and are completely made of glass. Only the WC has the appropriate privacy. It lies behind opaque glass walls, which also accommodate storage space and a kitchenette. The overhanging roof provides shade, and for additional protection curtains can be closed around the surrounding veranda. Solar panels and photovoltaic cells on the roof provide electricity and hot water, and a water tank and filtration system ensure drinking water.

The glass used is a high-performance triple-glazed insulating glass with a solar and heat protective coating. It blocks 75% of solar radiation but is extremely translucent with good thermal insulation properties. This makes it possible to maintain pleasant conditions within the building during all seasons in an energy-efficient and environmentally friendly way.

OLIVE TREE HOUSE

Halkidiki, Greece
Eva Sopéoglou

21 m²

226 ft²

Halkidiki is located in the north-east of Greece. Hikers, beach enthusiasts and amateur archaeologists alike enjoy coming to the peninsula, whose headlands extend like fingers into the Aegean Sea. The area is also famous for its agricultural products, including wine, honey and olive oil. It was an olive grove that inspired the Greek-British architect Eva Sopéoglou to create a weekend retreat and summer cottage.

A retired couple from Thessaloniki wanted a refuge from the busy life of the city. The ideal site is situated on a hill covered with olive trees with views of the sea and the famous monasteries on Mount Athos. The house was to be a simple temporary accommodation, with as little maintenance as possible. The architect designed a sleek rectangular structure, carefully adapted to the views, surrounding vegetation, prevailing winds and arc of the sun. Its façade is made of metal panels into which a detailed pattern inspired by the surrounding grove has been cut out with a CNC milling machine. Depending on the position of the sun,

the perforations throw changing shadows into the interior of the house like the canopy of leaves on a tree. In addition, the openings allow air to circulate. The modular walls are movable and can be unfolded to connect the inside and outside and extend the living space onto the terrace. At the highest point of the unilaterally sloping roof, there are ventilation openings through which upward rising heat can dissipate. They are accented with colour and cast bright spots of light on the walls and floor. Inside, instead of dividing walls, there are metal cupboards which provide requisite storage space.

The house skilfully incorporates its surroundings and, with its greenish colour scheme, blends harmoniously in with the natural colour palette. In addition, it can be dismantled at any time without leaving any major traces.

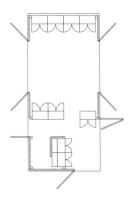

GARAGE CONVERSION

Vilnius, Lithuania
IM Interior

21 m²

226 ft²

It doesn't always have to be a new building. The conversion of existing structures is increasingly important. The way in which a former garage can be transformed into a modern, comfortable one-room flat with a small bathroom is wonderfully demonstrated by Indrė Mylytė-Sinkevičienė of IM Interior. She added a new façade of weathered steel to the original building located in historical Old Town of the Lithuanian capital. With its rust-red colour, it stands out against the neighbouring buildings, but its industrial appearance also allows it to fit in well with the mixed-use district. The designer furthermore provided the building with new openings, which were adapted to the spatial functions of the interior.

Living, sleeping and working areas, as well as the kitchen, are accommodated in a single large room. The patterned tiles on the floor in the middle and the slightly lowered ceilings with embedded LED lighting subtly define the different zones. Only the tiny bathroom with a toilet and shower is separated. The entire interior is designed with birch plywood, which gives

the tiny house a bright and welcoming atmosphere. Two horizontal windows frame views of the neighbouring house and the surrounding greenery. The bed, which also serves as a seat by the window, is fitted with drawers and cupboards to provide necessary storage space. In front of the second window runs a narrow tabletop that serves as both a dining table and desk.

With this project, the designer wanted to show how little one needs to live and how a different lifestyle is possible in a small space. Mission accomplished.

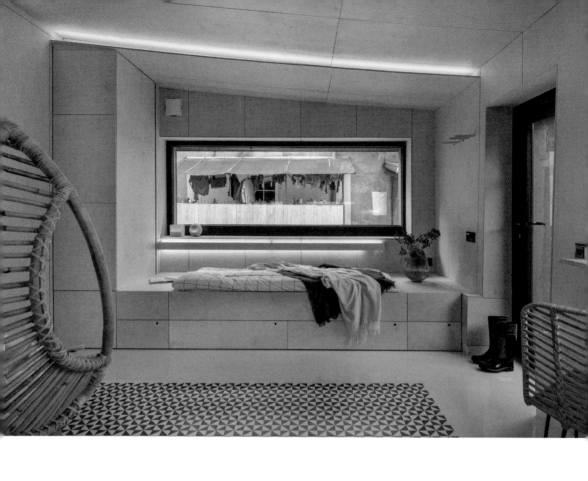

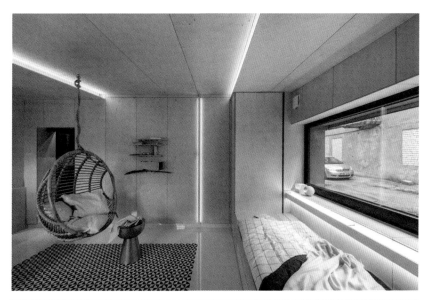

PANORAMA GLASS LODGE

Hella, Iceland
ÖÖD

23 m²

248 ft²

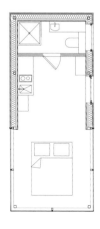

Geysers, fjords and waterfalls, glaciers, volcanoes and hot springs – adventurers and outdoor enthusiasts as well as natural scientists swoon over the diversity of Iceland's natural sights and spectacular settings. And, without doubt, the hope of catching a glimpse of the aurora borealis, or northern lights, is on the list of every traveller north. What could be a more comfortable way of doing this than simply lying in bed? This is exactly what Panorama Glass Lodge offers in southern Iceland, near Reykjavík.

The Estonian company ÖÖD, founded by brothers Andreas and Jaak Tiik, specialises in small houses. The prefabricated accommodations in Iceland are tailored to the specifications of the owners, a German-Swiss couple, and the local conditions. Despite the reduced size, the cottages offer every necessary amenity. Natural wood combined with dark surfaces create a cosy atmosphere. The décor is influenced by Viking culture and Nordic mythology; the octagonal tiles are a reference to the basalt columns found in Iceland. The copper roof resists the acid rain caused by the volcanic activity on the island, while adequate thermal insulation and triple glazing ensure a comfortable living environment in the harsh climate.

Visually and spatially, the refuges consist of two parts – a "practical" area comprising kitchenette, dining area and bathroom, with hardly any window openings and clad with wood on the outside, and a second part with "wow effect": the panoramic glass-walled bedroom. Here, the boundaries between inside and outside are blurred, the view extends far over the captivating vistas, and you experience sunrise and sunset, the starry sky and the polar lights directly from bed with an unobstructed view in all directions. Maximum peace and relaxation are guaranteed here!

CABANON CONCRETE RETREAT

Kissamos, Crete, Greece

Batakis Architects; Sofia Mavroudis + Antonis Choudalakis

32 m²

344 ft²

Rethink what luxury is – with two small concrete buildings, Greek artist Antonis Choudalakis and Swedish curator Sofia Mavroudis aim to offer a new impetus for exactly that. They see the two lodgings as a continuation of their existing artistic practice in which they attach great importance to local context and an interaction with nature. They find their particular take on luxury in a simple Cretan lifestyle, with its focus on the essential things in life: taking time, nurturing relationships, feeling the wind from the sea, looking up at the starry sky and sometimes simply doing nothing.

For this purpose, they have created a wonderful place with their accommodations in the northwest of Crete. They were inspired by Le Corbusier's famous wooden cabin Le Cabanon on the French Riviera. The retreats are kept minimalist and fit perfectly into the rough beauty of the surrounding olive groves. Everything superfluous – both in terms of space and furnishings – has been left out. The interior consists of a single room with a few steps dividing the living and cooking area from the raised sleeping area. Only the bathroom is separated. The furniture is also restrained and was predominantly made for the space by local craftsmen. Finally, the room is complemented by a little chic wood-burning stove, which provides pleasant warmth on those occasions when it gets cooler on the sunny Greek island. A fully glazed façade facing north-west allows endless views over the surrounding countryside and the coast and connects the space with nature.

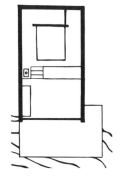

BLACKBIRD BYRON

Mullumbimby Creek, New South Wales, Australia
James and Stella Hudson

36–41 m²

388–441 ft²

The seaside resort of Byron Bay lies south of Brisbane at the easternmost point of mainland Australia. Its long beaches and turquoise waters attract both foreign tourists and local holidaymakers. The area is especially popular with surfers, and with many artists and downshifters drawn here, the place has gained something of a hippie reputation. Somewhat inland, amidst green, densely overgrown hills, James and Stella Hudson have created a special sanctuary. The industrial designer and interior designer moved from the big city of Sydney to the countryside, where they made a dream come true with the small bed and breakfast. Three elongated, shipping-container-like boxes serve as guest rooms. The layout is simple – in the front of the accommodation is the living and sleeping area, while a wall, which does not quite reach the height of the room, separates the entrance area and a small kitchenette, as well as the adjoining, enclosed bathroom. White varnished birch plywood defines the minimalist character of the room. Moroccan patterned tiles in the bathroom provide a more playful note, and the exposed pipework on the wall adds an industrial flair to the mix. A large window with adjustable glass louvres introduces light and air into the rear of the space.

The external cladding of fibre cement panels combined with rusted grids of metal mesh create a raw, industrial look. As a contrast, the Oriental pattern of the Moroccan tiles is repeated in the outdoor seating area.

The Hudsons are committed to running their B. & B. in the most environmentally friendly way possible. Electricity is provided by a solar array, and they grow their own fruit and vegetables and make their own soap. Recycled materials were used in the construction to keep resource consumption low. Wood from an old storage shed, for example, was used for the separate communal area, and reused railway sleepers frame wide views beyond the guest rooms of the green surroundings, Cape Byron and the Pacific Ocean.

BOOKWORM CABIN

near Adelin, Poland

Bartłomiej Kraciuk and Marta Puchalska-Kraciuk; POLE Architekci

37 m²

398 ft²

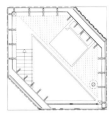

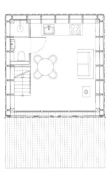

It's probably the dream of every bookworm, being able to indulge their pleasure for reading undisturbed in a cosy retreat, surrounded by book-lined shelves. The entrepreneur Bartłomiej Kraciuk and his wife, the architect Marta Puchalska-Kraciuk, have made this dream come true. Based on a slightly modified design by POLE Architekci, the two have built a weekend house only 40 minutes by car from Warsaw, in the middle of nature, surrounded by trees and fields.

The house is built entirely of wood: spruce for the wooden structure, roof and deck, pine boards for the interior and exterior panelling and oak for the floors. Space is limited, but with its partial sleeping loft, the cabin offers more space than you might expect from the outside. A small kitchenette and the bathroom located under the stairs fulfil their essential functions. But the core elements are, of course, the open living room with comfortable seating and the shelves that run along the walls and up to the roof, filled with reading material. A wood-burning stove provides a snug

atmosphere, while a generous amount of light comes in through the complete, almost 5-metre (16.5-foot)-high façade of glass. If you lift your eyes from the page and allow them to wander over the landscape outside, you might have the feeling of sitting in the middle of the forest. Huge wooden shutters provide protection when away and more privacy at night.

As the owners do not always have time to use their retreat themselves, they have decided to rent out the Bookworm Cabin. In this way more people can enjoy its peaceful tranquillity and just sit back and relax. With or without a book.

PAN-TRETOPPHYTTER

Gjesåsen, Hedmark, Norway
Espen Surnevik

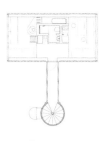

Finnskogen – Forest of the Finns – is the name of the hilly, wooded landscape in south-eastern Norway near the Swedish border. The name originated in the 17th century when Finnish emigrants settled the region. When the clients Kristian Rostad and Christine Mowinckel commissioned the Oslo architect Espen Surnevik to build two holiday homes in this area, he sought inspiration to develop a singular architecture that would pay tribute to the landscape and surrounding nature. He found it in the Finnish-Swedish writer and illustrator Tove Jansson and her mythical Nordic world populated by the Moomins, the hippo-like trolls she created. He was also inspired by the fire lookout towers rising high among the trees, which are used to spy out forest fires in good time.

And, thus, two Treetop Cabins were created consisting of a filigree steel construction on which an A-frame shelter is enthroned at a height of 8 metres (about 26 feet). This is reached via a cylindrical stair tower, which is connected to the cabin by a short footbridge. The structure, raised off the ground, creates a

sense of security and has hardly any impact on the landscape. The black steel in combination with the black oxidised zinc coating of the roof and the black window frames lend the building's exterior a rather technical appearance. The interior, in contrast, is lined with natural pine. Black accents, such as the kitchen, the wood-burning stove and the stairs to the sleeping area, echo the colour on the outside. Each cabin has room to sleep six – two bunk beds that can be folded out of the wall and a double bed that can be found in the loft. Thanks to thermal insulation and underfloor heating, you can enjoy your stay even in the winter months.

The PAN cabins look like geometric trees and fit perfectly into their surroundings. They show that modern architecture and nature do not have to be in opposition but can harmonise wonderfully.

CASA DE MONTE

Yucatán, Mexico
TACO taller de arquitectura contextual

42 m²

452 ft²

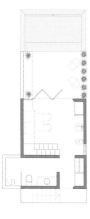

The Yucatán Peninsula separates the Gulf of Mexico from the Caribbean Sea. In its north-western point lies the Mexican state of the same name, which is home to some of the most important ruins of the Mayan civilisation. Architects at TACO were commissioned to build a small holiday home here for a couple on a plot of land covered with vegetation typical of the region's savannahs. It was intended to be a place to relax, both functional and simple, linked to the natural surroundings. The result is a house which stands on a platform and is aligned in such a way that the sun does not heat it too intensely, while cooling winds ensure pleasant temperatures within. As it would have been difficult to excavate a foundation in the rocky terrain, the building's elevated position allows for a swimming pool sunk into the platform. A tree which was already growing there provides shade. The terrace at the front extends the living space to the outside. Directly inside, a small kitchen and living area occupy a room two-storeys tall. At the rear, a so-called samba staircase, with treads alternating from left to right, leads to the elevated sleeping area. Below this is the bathroom with an outdoor shower and a storage room.

Clean lines and simple geometric cubes dominate the design, from the outer appearance of the building to the steps of the staircase. The uniform materiality with rough stucco connects the interior with the exterior. The wooden shutters made of cedar on the sleeping loft and facing the terrace provide a contrast. The angle of daylight can be controlled by means of adjustable louvres. The walls are painted with a traditionally produced paint made of lime and mineral pigments and the interior decorations were carefully crafted by hand. In this way, the minimalist house distracts as little as possible from an enjoyment of the unspoilt natural environment.

SUSTAINABLE HOUSE

Ouro Branco, Minas Gerais, Brazil

Gustavo Penna Arquiteto & Associados

The Brazilian state of Minas Gerais has been the largest mining centre in Brazil since colonial times. In the past, gold, diamonds and other gemstones were mined there, but since the Industrial Age, iron ore, zinc and phosphate minerals are some of the resources now being extracted. In collaboration with a large Brazilian steel company and the Department of Mining Engineering at the Federal University of Minas Gerais in Belo Horizonte, architect Gustavo Penna has designed a house that incorporates mining waste in the construction, using it to replace conventional building materials. The pilot project is located on the grounds of the Biocentro Germinar, where environmental education is offered to children and adolescents from the neighbouring communities. It is intended to shine a light on the possibilities of recycling management and more sustainable construction.

The house is built of concrete blocks, which were produced using residual minerals left over by the mining process. The stones are left visible both inside and out, giving the building an industrial

appearance. This is reinforced by the concrete floors, exposed pipes running along the walls and the simple, unadorned furniture.

The design takes into account a number of energy-efficient and climate-friendly strategies. These include the solar thermal system on the roof for heating water, photovoltaic panels for generating electricity and the use of rainwater. Other measures have been taken under consideration but were determined only to be worthwhile for larger housing developments, such as burning waste for energy or a domestic biogas plant. The structure's dynamic sculptural form also plays a role – the towering stretch of wall was born from the idea of installing a wind generator at the top of the large recess to generate energy. The large glass façade uses solar radiation for passive heating, while the gently projecting roof protects against overheating. It was also important to ensure sufficient natural ventilation. At the same time, however, the architect's aim was to create a house in which the residents would feel at home, regardless of the many functional considerations.

THE HIDE

Callestick, Cornwall, Great Britain

Jess Clark and Sarah Stanley/Unique Homestays; Studio Arc

46 m²

495 ft²

The county of Cornwall in southwest England is known for its beautiful gardens, impressive castles, rugged coasts and picturesque bays with fine sandy beaches. Close to popular Perranporth Beach and Holywell Bay, a vacation home with a minimalist design has been built a little way inland from the Atlantic. Surfaces of *béton brut*, or exposed concrete, characterise both the exterior and interior of the house, combined with untreated, natural wood. This may convey the charm of a simple life in the country, but despite the small space this hideaway offers every creature comfort you could wish for. The clear design with its restrained colour palette is unobtrusive while managing to harmonise with the natural surroundings. This effect is achieved, for example, through the large windows, whose glass panes slope outwards over the façade, extending the field of vision. The main room with its kitchenette and the living and dining area boast such a panoramic window, and the same "extended" glass panes are even placed at the head of the bed so that as soon as you open your eyes you are greeted with idyllic views. There is also a wide French door onto the terrace that connects the interior with an exterior seating area and the naturally landscaped garden. Inside, the generous expanses of glass provide an abundance of light and a welcoming atmosphere.

The concrete design extends into the bathroom. Here, both the bathtub and washbasin are cast from the same grey material. Embrasure-like openings allow light to enter the room. On the outside, this part of the house in which the more private rooms are located is clad with wooden shingles. Since these are exposed to wind and weather, the wood has begun to turn grey, taking on a silver patina over the years.

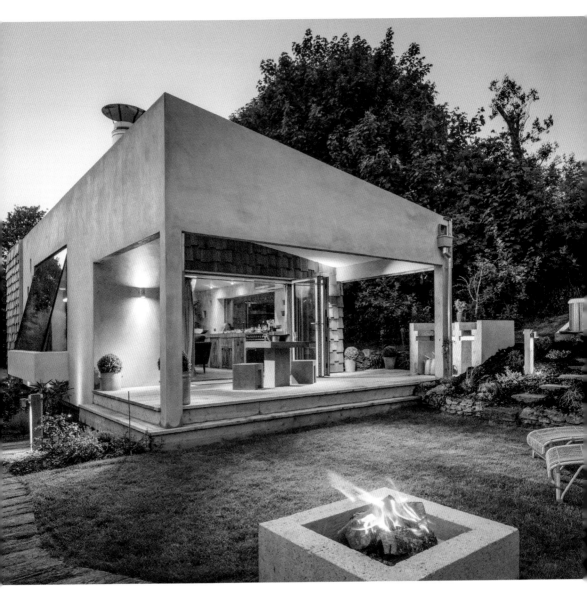

APAN PROTOTYPE

Apan, Hidalgo, Mexico

Dellekamp Arquitectos – Derek Dellekamp and Jachen Schleich

52 m²

560 ft²

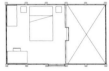

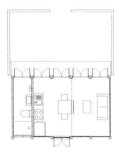

A single-family home, beautiful and functional, flexible in use, easy to expand, durable and inexpensive to build – this was the brief given to participating architects for the study Laboratorio de Vivienda – the "housing laboratory". The aim was to find new ideas for social housing. As part of the programme, 32 prototypes, planned by Latin American architects, were built on a test site in the Mexican city of Apan. The houses meet the requirements by using an open concept and an architecture based on Mexican building traditions, using easily available building materials including brick, corrugated metal, concrete and wood. There was no need to reinvent the art of construction, instead participants were expected skilfully to apply proven methods to build affordable houses that suit the climate. This is achieved by using features such as modular construction, moveable elements and passive cooling. Ideally, residents can even build their houses themselves.

Derek Dellekamp and Jachen Schleich designed a two-storey building made entirely of wood. The modular structure uses local softwood, a readily available resource and common to construction in the region. This allows for easy assembly. On the lower level there is room to accommodate living, eating and cooking, as well as the bath. A ladder leads up to the sleeping loft. This also ensures spatial differentiation, as the living room is two storeys high, reaching to the roof, while the area under the loft is lower. The plywood wall covering and the exposed beams give the interior a somewhat raw but homely atmosphere. A narrow outdoor area may be found along one of the longer sides. Here, the façade can be completely opened by means of folding doors, extending the space outwards. The prototypes have all been furnished with two specially developed furniture lines by Mexican designer Héctor Esrawe.

GRANNY PAD

Seattle, Washington, USA
Best Practice Architecture

53 m²

571 ft²

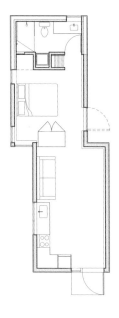

What can you do when you want to have your aging parents close by, but there's just no more room in your own house and you still need a bit of privacy? One family in Seattle was lucky: In their garden there was an old garage that was being used as a storage shed. The architects of Best Practice Architecture saw it as the perfect starting point for a self-contained granny flat. They extended the original space by adding a second, slightly offset building to create a small house with a total of 53 square metres (571 square feet). All rooms are on one level and accessible without having to step over any thresholds – an important prerequisite for comfortable living for any elderly person. One enters the house directly through the open kitchen-dining room and living area, which fill the former garage. The bedroom behind is separated spatially by a single chest of drawers. The only closed room in the house is the spacious bathroom with a walk-in shower and washing machine. A steep ladder leads up to a small loft, which is currently used as storage space. But if needed, it could

be converted into another sleeping area or an office. This upper level also takes advantage of the slight incline on which the building is situated, with a door leading directly into the garden. A generous amount of daylight enters the space through carefully placed large windows and several skylights. Throughout the house, the sloping roof is visible inside, and in some cases the load-bearing beams are also exposed. The resulting double height of the room, in combination with the light plywood panelling on the walls and ceilings, the white plaster and light grey concrete floor, create a large, open environment. In contrast, the exterior of the house forms a uniform black cube with dark stained cedar and roof tiles of the same hue. A splash of colour is provided by the pink front door, intended to welcome visitors.

CHALET

Donovaly, Slovakia
Y100 ateliér

689 ft²

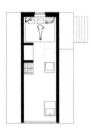

Donovaly is situated within Low Tatras National Park. It is one of the most well-known ski resorts in Slovakia and is also famous as a venue for sled dog racing. The architects' goal was not to create a building that competes with the natural beauty of the surroundings but rather one which blends harmoniously into the dense forest on the property. The original cabin, which was built in the 1970s, was run-down but stable enough to be renovated, with some parts of the structure preserved. It was to remain simple yet offer a certain amount of comfort. In order to make the area under the sloping roof, which extends to the floor, feel more spacious, Jana Štofan Styková and Pavol Štofan from Y100 ateliér removed one of the bedrooms on the upper floor. Subsequently, an open, two-storey living and dining room with a wood-burning stove was created behind the fully glazed front. Behind is the kitchen, as well as the foyer and bathroom. From the sunken tub it is possible to look directly into the forest through a window in the roof. A ladder

staircase leads up to the loft. There, kept next to essential storage space, are mattresses for four people. A rope net protects from falling. The interior is completely covered with OSB panels, which gives the rooms a raw yet homely charm. In contrast, the floorboards made of oak provide a more refined note. The roof and the window frames are covered in aluminium, and the door onto the deck stands out with its green frame. Two decks made of larch are connected by several steps and a slide. The name of the holiday home, chAlet, with its capital "A", plays on the name for this kind of roof-only construction – an "A-frame house".

THE SLOT HOUSE

London, Great Britain
Sandy Rendel Architects with Sally Rendel

64 m²

689 ft²

Between the buildings of many large cities there are often gaps which remain unused because nobody really knows what to do with such tiny spaces. But Sandy and Sally Rendel demonstrated how it is possible to build a small but attractive residential building in such a gap in the south-east London district of Peckham. They originally bought the plot – roughly the size of a carriage on the London Underground – to create a garden for their adjoining terraced house. Then, finding that they still had space left, they planned a two-storey house for the mere 2.80-metre (9.2-foot)-wide slot. In order to preserve as much space as possible and avoid the need to transfer weight across the neighbouring buildings, they opted for a lightweight steel structure, which was prefabricated in modules in a factory. They were then welded together on site. The grey-painted beams remain visible inside the house, and they are even occasionally used for built-in shelves. The steel elements are combined with sleek, natural materials, such as a continuous brick wall on the ground floor, spruce plywood for walls and ceilings, Douglas fir for the exposed ceiling beams and floors covered in cork or terrazzo.

In order to create a sense of spaciousness and to allow as much daylight as possible to enter the building, the interior is designed as a largely open space. You enter directly into the kitchen and dining area. The staircase positioned in the middle of the house with adjoining bathrooms separates the kitchen from the living room on the lower floor and the bedroom from the office on the upper floor. A skylight above the stairs lets light into the middle of the upper floor, while an open two-storey space behind the fully glazed garden façade connects the two levels. On the upper floor, the work area may be closed off with walls when necessary to create another bedroom. The architects hope that their design will inspire other architects and developers to undertake similar projects – highly desirable in these times when living space is sparse in large cities.

YURT

near Portland, Oregon, USA
Zach Both and Nicole Lopez

68 m²

730 ft²

Yurts are round tent dwellings mainly used by nomadic groups in the steppes of Central Asian, especially in Mongolia, Kyrgyzstan and Kazakhstan. A traditional yurt consists of a wooden frame covered with cotton and felt fabrics. The structure can be dismantled quickly and erected again elsewhere, which is important for the nomadic lifestyle. During the last few decades, however, yurts have gained popularity in other countries as well, and there are now several companies which implement this traditional concept, mostly using modern materials.

Filmmaker Zach Both had lived in a camper van for some time before he decided to settle down. But due to the high real estate prices in Portland, he and his girlfriend Nicole Lopez sought out alternatives and came across yurts. They ordered the shell of their new home from an American manufacturer, but the interior design was based entirely on their own ideas. With the help of friends and family, they were able to build the basic structure in just one weekend, consisting of a wood floor on a concrete foundation,

a wooden lattice for the walls and wooden beams with a central wooden ring as an anchor for the roof structure. Thermal insulation and a vinyl cover as an outer skin have been attached, as well as a central Plexiglass dome. The interior fittings were carried out by the couple themselves during months of DIY work. The result is a modern space with a restrained colour palette of black, white and light wood, interspersed with the green of their many plants. The couple also had the ingenious idea to place a rectangular cube in the middle of the round space containing the bathroom and kitchenette. On top, the two set up their comfortable "sleeping nest" surrounded by an array of plants.

In order to help others interested in building their own yurt, Zach Both shares his insights on the subject on his website, "DoItYurtself".

HOUSE ON AN ISLAND

Skåtøy, Norway
Atelier Oslo

70 m²

753 ft²

Skerry are small rocky islands formed during the ice ages. They owe their flat, rounded shape to the continental ice sheet which scraped over the rock and scoured it down. The island of Skåtøy is the largest skerry off Kragerø on the south coast of Norway. An artist couple commissioned the architects from Atelier Oslo to build a house on the water's edge that is skilfully adapted to the uneven topography and incorporates the surrounding rocks into its design. Access is from the rear and a staircase leads down through the house to the entrance at the front. Concrete floors run on several levels from the interior to the exterior. They eliminate the separation between living space and open space, while the surrounding floor-to-ceiling windows contribute to this effect and join the architecture as part of the landscape. Inside, the slightly staggered levels, connected by steps, create a spatial separation in the open concept. The structure of the house is made of Kebony wood, and it was prefabricated

and then assembled on site. The ceiling consist of exposed wooden beams, and the final layer of the roof is also made of wood. It extends downward as a grid in front of the glass façade and filters the incoming light, and thus creates patterns with shadows which are intended to evoke the calming feeling of sitting under a canopy of leaves. With time, the wooden structure is turning grey, causing it to match the colour of the concrete surfaces.

In the living room, something like a concrete sculpture rises up from the floor. It has several steps leading to a raised platform which is ideal for relaxing and, at the same time, the sculpture forms a bench with an integrated wood-burning stove. A cube, containing a kitchenette, bathroom and the utility room, is also made of concrete. The minimalist interior offers the two artists distraction-free space for their creative work, while the framed views and the natural effects of light provide inspiration.

189

SKINNY HOUSE

Tezukayama, Osaka, Japan
FujiwaraMuro Architects

73 m²

786 ft²

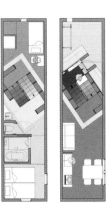

Plots of land in the centre of most big cities are expensive and scarce. One reaction to this issue, which is particularly common in Japan, is *infill* – to build extremely narrow "gap fillers" or buildings located on a plot of land only a few metres wide, often wedged between existing structures. Inspired designs emerge out of these challenging conditions again and again, managing to make a virtue of necessity and use the available space in clever and innovative ways.

In the case of this Skinny House in Tezukayama, in the Japanese prefecture of Osaka, the architects were already involved in the search for a building plot. In the end, they decided on a section of land in a densely built-up area, 3.74-metres (12-feet)-wide and 16.31-metres (53.5-feet)-deep. In order to create as much usable space as possible in the limited area, FujiwaraMuro Architects developed a central architectural element which redefines the idea of a stairwell: the steps with surrounding shelves are simultaneously designed as a place to

lounge and play, a storage unit and a workspace. The structure, which spirals through the space, connects the various levels of the house, designed as split levels – one with a bedroom and a bathroom; another which can be used as a children's room, guest room or study; the living, dining and cooking area; the workstation which is integrated into the "shelf stairwell"; and finally, to finish off, a small roof terrace.

Only the bathroom has interior walls, otherwise the wooden structure in the middle of the house defines the spatial separation of the building's individual parts. Because the neighbourhood is rather unsightly, window openings are sparse. Daylight enters mainly from above, and panes of glass are integrated into the floor around the shelf-stairs, allowing light to reach the lower floors. The stairwell's versatility transforms it from a mere passageway into the "pivotal hub" of family life, in the truest sense of the phrase.

H3 HOUSE

Mar Azul, Argentina

Luciano Kruk

The small settlement of Mar Azul on the Atlantic Coast, south of Buenos Aires, is located on the water in a landscape of dunes divided into an even, rectangular grid. Old pine trees offer shade and lend the village a certain charm. Here, three sisters commissioned the architect Luciano Kruk, known for his purist concrete buildings, to construct a holiday home for themselves and their families. The result is a concrete structure with large surfaces of glass, in which nature and living space seem to flow into each other. The trees on the property pleasantly filter the incoming light through the floor-to-ceiling windows. The compact floor plan allows for relaxing, dining and cooking on the ground floor. On the floor above are two bedrooms and a bathroom. In order to make the limited space appear larger, the rooms are openly connected, offering views through the whole house to the outside and, via the open staircase, also to the upper level.

The entire building is constructed using *béton brut*, or exposed concrete, a durable and low-maintenance material. Every surface clearly shows the wood grain of the concrete formwork, providing a mental association with the surrounding trees. Even some of the furniture is cast in concrete and directly integrated into the structure of the summer house, further promoting the feel of a flowing spatial continuum. The cement grey is complemented by the black of the furniture, kitchen appliances and steel frames of the windows – a minimalist choice of material that would certainly not meet everyone's idea of comfortable vacation architecture. The deck behind the house and the balcony connected to the bedrooms, however, bring warmer tones into the mix with their wood panelling.

YŌ NO IE

Isumi, Chiba, Japan
Muji

80 m²

861 ft²

The Japanese lifestyle brand Muji (short for "Mujirushi Ryōhin", which roughly translates as "no-brand quality goods") has been producing prefabricated houses for several years now, which have until recently been multi-storey buildings more designed for urban or suburban settings. With the "Plain House" Yō no Ie, these choices have been supplemented by a single-storey variant which keeps country life in mind and is also suitable for older people thanks to its stepless, barrier-free floor plan. Like the other houses from the Japanese company, the compact layout has no interior walls and consists of only one room, conveying a sense of spaciousness. Residents can furnish and use the space freely, and it can be easily adapted over time to changing needs and living situations. Buildings in Japan are often not designed to last, but Muji's houses are all characterised by solid, earthquake-proof construction, high-quality materials and good thermal insulation.

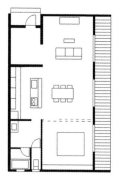

One focus of the Plain House is the relationship between interior and exterior space. The level deck stretches across the entire width of the house and seamlessly connects the living space to the outdoors through the large, floor-to-ceiling sliding doors. The narrow porch is reminiscent of the *engawa*, a kind of veranda or outdoor corridor, typical of traditional Japanese homes. It also serves to protect the interior from the intense angle of the summer sun. The selection of materials used in the structure is dominated by different types of wood: The exterior of the building is clad with Japanese chestnut, the deck is made of cedar, and the floors are made of oak planks. Together with the smooth white walls, the resulting appearance is simple and clean. Yō no Ie can be constructed in a range of sizes, from configurations of about 65 to 110 square metres (700 to 1,184 square feet). They are, however, currently only available in Japan.

EX OF IN HOUSE

Rhinebeck, New York, USA

Steven Holl Architects

85 m²

918 ft²

Initially, a typical suburban development – like those in other parts of the USA, or indeed the rest of the world – was planned for these 11 hectares (27 acres) of land in New York State. However, instead of permitting further urban sprawl, the area was ultimately made a nature preserve. Now there stands a rather modest building with 85 square metres (918 square feet) of living space over two storeys, which serves as a guest house and artist retreat. The architect Steven Holl designed the structure based on his architectural-philosophical reflections on the preposition "in" – hence the name of the house, "Explorations of In" – regarding the spatial language and energy of buildings in connection with their surroundings.

The resulting building consists of interlocking geometric shapes and geometric forms cut out of them. Thus, you enter the house through an empty spherical space that opens into the spacious main room, characterised by its sloping walls and ceilings. The living, kitchen and dining areas are separated from each other by several steps. In the loft is an office, along with possible space to sleep. Officially, the house does not have any bedrooms, but it is possible for up to five adults to sleep there. One of the beds is found on top of the "entrance orb", one of the many places in the building which impressively illustrate the architect's play with space and form. Great importance was given to the choice of materials: Natural materials such as finished mahogany and birch plywood define the interior. The lamps made of bioplastic produced from corn starch were created using a 3D printer.

In terms of energy, the house is entirely self-sufficient thanks to geothermal heating and a photovoltaic system with battery storage. The façade openings are all aligned to different sun elevations, capturing the morning sun in the east and the sunset over the Hudson Valley in the west. On the south side, a circular cut-out marks the midday sun. The connection between architecture and the surrounding outdoors has been exceptionally implemented here.

ARCHITECTS + DESIGNERS

Fernando Abellanas
Valencia, Spain
lebrel.org

Atelier Oslo
Oslo, Norway
atelieroslo.no

Au Workshop
Budapest, Hungary
auworkshop.com

Base Cabin
Melbourne, Australia
basecabin.com

Batakis Architects
Chania, Crete, Greece
batakis-construction.com

Best Practice Architecture
Seattle, Washington, USA
bestpracticearchitecture.com

BMCO Product Design
Zurich, Switzerland
bmco.ch

Zach Both
Portland, Oregon, USA
doityurtself.com

Build Tiny
Wellington, New Zealand
buildtiny.co.nz

**Jess Clark and Sarah
Stanley/Unique Homestays**
Newquay, Cornwall, Great Britain
uniquehomestays.com

Dellekamp Arquitectos
Mexico City, Mexico
dellekamparq.com

Leonardo Di Chiara
Pesaro, Italy
leonardodichiara.it

El Sindicato Arquitectura
Quito, Ecuador
elsindicatoarquitectura.com

First Light Studio
Wellington, New Zealand
firstlightstudio.co.nz

Format Engineers
Bath, Great Britain
formatengineers.com

FujiwaraMuro Architects
Osaka, Japan
aplan.jp

HANNAH Design Office
Ithaca, New York, USA
hannah-office.org

Steven Holl Architects
New York, USA
stevenholl.com

IM Interior
Vilnius, Lithuania
iminterior.lt

KOOP Architects and Engineers
Weimar, Germany
koop-hc.de

KOOP Mobile Timber Constructions
Blankenhain, Germany
koop-mhs.de

Luciano Kruk
Buenos Aires, Argentina
lucianokruk.com

L'Abri
Montreal, Quebec, Canada
labri.ca

Sjaak Langenberg & Rosé de Beer
's-Hertogenbosch, Netherlands
sjaaklangenberg.nl
rosedebeer.nl

MINI Living
Munich, Germany
mini.com/en_MS/home/living.html
bmwgroup.com

Muji
Tokyo, Japan
muji.net/ie

ÖÖD
Tallinn, Estonia
oodhouse.com

OFIS Arhitekti
Ljubljana, Slovenia
ofis.si

On Running
Zurich, Switzerland
on-running.com

OPEN Architecture
Beijing, China
openarch.com

penda China
Beijing, China
penda-china.com

Gustavo Penna Arquiteto & Associados
Belo Horizonte, Brazil
gustavopenna.com.br

POLE Architekci
Warsaw, Poland
polearchitekci.pl

Marta Puchalska-Kraciuk
Warsaw, Poland
moszczynskapuchalska.com

Refunc
The Hague, Netherlands
refunc.nl

Sandy Rendel Architects
London, Great Britain
sandyrendel.com

Eva Sopéoglou
London, Great Britain
evasopeoglou.com

SPINN Arkitekter
Oslo, Norway
spinnark.no

Studio Arc
Truro, Cornwall, Great Britain
studio-arc.co.uk

Studio Edwards
Melbourne, Australia
studio-edwards.com

Espen Surnevik
Oslo, Norway
espensurnevik.no

TACO taller de arquitectura contextual
Mérida, Mexico
arquitecturacontextual.com

Jan Tyrpekl
Strančice, Czech Republic
jantyrpekl.com

The Way We Build
Amsterdam, Netherlands
thewaywebuild.com

Y100 ateliér
Banská Bystrica, Slovakia
y100.sk

HOUSES FOR RENT

Blackbird Byron
Mullumbimby Creek, New South
Wales, Australia
blackbirdbyron.com.au

Bookworm Cabin
near Adelin, Poland
bookwormcabin.eu

Cabanon Concrete Retreat
Kissamos, Crete, Greece
cabanonconcreteretreat.com

Ex of In House
Rhinebeck, New York, USA
airbnb.com/rooms/21409981

Forest Cabin
Slootdorp, Netherlands
hetbosroept.nl/nl/accommodaties/
data/forest-cabin/#verblijf

The Hide
Callestick, Cornwall, Great Britain
uniquehomestays.com/self-catering/
uk/cornwall/perranporth/the-hide/

Hortus Hermitage
Haren (Groningen), Netherlands
hortusharen.nl/en/hortus-
hermitage-5

Hytte No. 1
Blankenhain, Germany
campingplatz-hohenfelden.de/de/
tiny%20house-hytte

PAN-tretopphytter
Gjesåsen, Hedmark, Norway
panhytter.no

Panorama Glass Lodge
Hella, Iceland
panoramaglasslodge.com

Refuge Le Pic mineur
Poisson Blanc Regional Park,
Quebec, Canada
poissonblanc.ca/experiences/
refuge-de-la-pointe-a-la-truite

THE AUTHOR

Sandra Leitte is an architect and has worked as a contributing editor on numerous publications regarding architecture, design and art. As an author, she has written books on tiny houses and houseboats. She divides her time between North Dakota, USA, and Munich, Germany.

© Prestel Verlag, Munich · London · New York 2021, 2022
A member of Penguin Random House Verlagsgruppe GmbH
Neumarkter Strasse 28 · 81673 Munich

A CIP catalogue record for this book is available from the
British Library.

Editorial direction Prestel: Sabine Schmid
Translation: Noel Zmija-Maurice
Copyediting: José Enrique Macián
Design and layout: Sofarobotnik, Augsburg & Munich
Production management: Andrea Cobré
Separations: Schnieber Graphik, Munich
Printing and binding: DZS grafik, Ljubljana, Slovenia
Paper: Primaset 170 g/m²

Penguin Random House Verlagsgruppe FSC® N001967
Printed in Slovenia
ISBN 978-3-7913-8723-9
www.prestel.com

PICTURE CREDITS

Front Cover: Bookworm Cabin, see pp. 132–137,
photo: Piotr Bednarski
Back Cover: Hammerfest Hiking Cabins, see pp. 46–51,
photo: Tor Even Mathisen

pp. 11, 13 Tamás Bujnovszky · p. 12 Au Workshop · pp. 15–17 Jose
Manuel Pedrajas · pp. 19, 21 below Gianluca Fiore · pp. 20, 23
Leonardo Di Chiara · p. 21 above Anna Fontanet Castillo · p. 22 Stefan
Dauth · pp. 25, 26 below right, 27, 29 Andy Chen · p. 26 above right, 28
HANNAH Design Office · p. 26 left Reuben Chen · pp. 31, 33–35 Wu
Qingshan · p. 32 Nácasa & Partners Inc. · pp. 37, 39 left, 40, 41 Andrés
Villota – Andres.V.Fotografia · p. 38 Paolo Caicedo · p. 39 right El
Sindicato Arquitectura · pp. 43–45 Antonín Matějovský · pp. 47–51 Tor
Even Mathisen · pp. 53–55, 56 left, 57 Anne Lutz & Thomas Stöckli ·
p. 56 above and below right Damian Schneider · pp. 59, 61, 63 below
Ishka Michocka · pp. 60, 62, 63 above Ben Nienhuis · pp. 65–68 Tom
Ross · p. 69 Felix Bardot · pp. 71–73 Jordi Huisman · pp. 75–79 Jack
Jérôme · pp. 81, 83, 84 Laurian Ghinitoiu/© Courtesy of BMW Group ·
pp. 82, 85 Xia Zhi/© Courtesy of BMW Group · pp. 87–89 Cassandra
Sharp Photography/© Build Tiny Limited · pp. 91–95 Lotta Heise ·
pp. 97–100 Gonzalo Botet/© Courtesy of Guardian Glass · p. 101 José
Navarrete · pp. 103–107 Mariana Bisti · pp. 109–113 Leonas
Garbačauskas · pp. 115–119 Panorama Glass Lodge Iceland · pp. 121–
125 Alpha Smoot · pp. 127–131 Saul Goodwin, Property Shot
Photography · pp. 133, 134, 136 Piotr Bednarski · pp. 135, 137 Ernest
Wińczyk · pp. 139–141 Rasmus Norlander · pp. 143–146 Leo Espinosa ·
p. 147 Alejandro Patrón · pp. 149–153 Jomar Bragança · pp. 155–159
Unique Homestays, uniquehomestays.com · pp. 161–165 Jaime
Navarro · pp. 167–169 Ed Sozinho · pp. 171–174 Miro Pochyba · p. 175
Pavol Stofan · pp. 177–181 Jim Stephenson · pp. 183–187 Bryan Aulick ·
pp. 189–191, 193–195 Ivar Kvaal · p. 192 Nils Vik · pp. 197–201 Toshiyuki
Yano Photography · pp. 203–209 Daniela Mac Adden · pp. 211–213
Muji · pp. 215–219 Paul Warchol Photography